I0191212

Letter 6:
Jesus Was a
Rabbi—OMG!

by Leonard Swidler

About iPubCloud.com

iPubCloud.com is the Digital Publishing arm of iPub Global Connection, LLC. Focusing on globally transformative books from authors all over the world, we value and help promote the works of creators who influence our world in matters of equality, interfaith dialogue, psychology, philosophy, and planet sustainability.

Our value to you is simplicity and convenience. The continually curated book list is culled from the New York Times, Amazon reader reviews, and iPub subject matter advisors. You may be confident when you select an item from our store; everything is fulfilled by Amazon, its affiliates, and other important distribution channels.

There are many books like this one on iPubCloud.com along with selections of other book categories. Don't keep us a secret. Connect with us on Facebook and join our mailing list. And, if you have a story to tell, reach out.

iPub Global Connection, LLC
https://www.iPubCloud.com
1050 W. Nido Ave., Mesa, AZ 85210
info@iPubCloud.com
Copyright © 2019 Leonard Swidler
Cover Design by Arewa Abiodun Ibrahim
ISBN-13: 978-1-948575-25-6
ISBN-13 ebook 978-1-948575-24-9

Other Books by Leonard Swidler may be found on *www.iPubCloud.com*

INTRODUCTION

"Will" is short for Willow Athena Swidler-Notte, my fantastic grand-daughter, born at the beginning of the Third Millennium (2000). I have been going to her home practically every weekend since 2011, to teach her German (which is why I am addressed as *Opa*, a typical German abbreviation for Grandpa). We talk about all kinds of interesting things in life—and end up having dinner with Will and my brilliant daughter Eva and her wonderful husband Ian. Both are professors, Ian, a high school ecology and biology teacher, and Eva, a university history teacher.

These are my letters to Will, with whom— when you meet her, you will understand why—I clearly am madly in love.

Len Swidler, (info@ipubcloud.com)

CONTENTS

Dear Will,

In my last letter to you, I noted to you that Jesus, the "Foundation" of Christianity, wasn't even a Christian, but was a Jew ! In a kind of throw-away remark you wrote back, "that's kinda weird." Then you added a quizzical question that has been itching in my brain since then: "Does it make any difference that Jesus was not Christian, but Jewish?"

1. WHO SHOULD BE INTERESTED IN WHETHER JESUS WAS A JEW?

Actually, Will, the more I thought about it, the more I became convinced that it wasn't really just a throw-away remark or flip question. It shines a light on a very deep and troubling--two-thousand-year-old problem.

Also, Will, yours is not a question that only Christians should follow up on! No, it is clear to me that most of the rest of the world should also probe the question. After all, Christians in 2010 numbered 2.2 billion out of a world total of 6.9 billion—almost a third of the global population! In that number of people who should be interested, Will, we should obviously include the global Jewish population of 15 million—precisely because Jesus was Jewish. In fact, he was the most influential Jew in all of history! (Runners-up would include Karl Marx, Sigmund Freud, and Albert Einstein.) Further, we should also include the 1.6 billion Muslims in the world, for the Qur'an reverently refers to Jesus (*Isa*) as the *al-Masih* (Messiah), and explicitly mentions with great respect his mother Mary (*Maryam*) more often than any other woman (in fact, the Qur'an even has a whole chapter named *Maryam*, after her!)

All these together make up almost 4 billion (roughly 70%) out of the total number of people living in 2010! So, Will, whether one is 1) a Christian (or *former* Christian—and perhaps especially them!), 2) a Jew, 3) a Muslim—4) an agnostic, or 5) even a "raving atheist," for most often they both are thus, consciously or not, rejecting the Christianity they grew up in, or around them—they should all care about Jesus. What Jesus thought of himself—and what his first followers thought of him—should be fundamental questions for them!

I hear you, Will; you are thinking: why should they care? Well, Will, in short--the modern world, for good and ill--has been massively formed and shaped by Western Civilization, which has as one of its core elements Christianity—built on Jesus of Nazareth—who wasn't even a Christian!

Will, in an earlier letter where we learned that "Jesus was a Feminist," I wrote that in the rest of that letter I was going to use the Hebrew form of Jesus' name, *Yeshua*, as a conscious help for us moderns to remember that he was not a Greek or a Roman (*Jesus* is the Latin form of the Greek *Iesous*, which in turn is a translation of the Hebrew *Yeshua*— meaning "God, *Yahweh*, saves"). He was a Jew!

2. GOD IS "ECHAD," ONE!

So, Will, what's one of the first things we think of when we think about Yeshua being a Jew and not a Greek or Roman? Well, Greeks and Romans, and everybody else, were polytheists; only the Jews claimed that there is just *one* source of everything that exists, including all humans. That means that despite all the differences among humans, as the very beginning of the Bible claims, all humans are to be treated with the *same* rules, for they all were created by the *same*, the *one* God. God is, as said in the most important Jewish prayer recited every day by devout Jews, *Echad, One*!

Shema Yisrael Yahweh Eloheinu Yahweh Echad!

Remember O Israel; Yahweh—our God Yahweh—is One!

3. CREATION IS "*TOV*," HUMANS ARE "*MOD TOV*"

And here's the clincher, Will; the very first book of the Bible states that at the end of each day of creation "God saw that what he had done was good" (*Tov* in Hebrew). Further, at the end of the sixth day, when God created humanity, the Bible states that "God saw that what he had done was "very good." (*Mod Tov*).

Now, Will, I can just hear you saying that millions of modern people don't think that the world was created in six days! True enough, Will. In fact, hundreds of millions of Christians don't either! The important point, Will, is that the vast majority of Western Europeans, most of whom were Christian, did until less than a couple of hundred years ago (1859, Charles Darwin's *Origin of Species*), and they shaped their (our!) civilization accordingly. That meant, Will, that the basic thrust of developing Christian/Western

Civilization had at its foundation the claim that *all* humans, precisely because they came from *one* (*Echad*) source, should be treated "very well," *Mod Tov*.

There are other ways, of course, to understand that all humans are the equivalent of *Mod Tov* than Biblical religion. But, Will, the important point here is that this idea that *all* humans are *Mod Tov* has been spread around the whole world in substantial ways by the followers of this Biblical religion; by Christians and their cultural descendants.

Again Will, I hear you thinking that an awful lot of so-called followers of the Bible, Christians, didn't follow that teaching at all! That is clearly still is true in 2019—one need only think of how the current president of our country horribly mistreats everyone different from him (clearly, he does not think that any non-white Christians are even *Tov*, let alone, *Mod Tov*!—and is still followed by millions of so-called "evangelical," (from the Greek of the New Testament, *Evangelion*, "Gospel"?!) Christians. Those "Others" clearly are not seen by these Christians as *Mod Tov*!

Nevertheless, Will, hundreds of millions of other Christians do follow, for example, the banner of Pope Francis (and not just Catholics) in constantly urging care and concern for multiple others, especially the poor and oppressed, for they indeed are *Mod Tov*.

Hence, both the Christians and the rest of the world need to attend to the fact that the fundamental teaching—and example—of Rabbi Yeshua was essentially *Jewish* when he reached out to and treated especially the sick, poor, and marginalized (women, *Jesus Was a Feminist!*) as *Mod Tov*, indeed.

4. RABBI YESHUA WAS MOST INTERESTED IN SOCIETY'S MARGINALIZED OUTCASTS

One of the greatest contributions Western Civilization, the "offspring" of Christendom, has made to the whole world is the notion, and growing reality, of human rights, essentially meaning that all humans are to be treated as *Mod Tov*! Yes, Will, it took a long, long time for Westerners (including Christians!) to realize that all humans came from one Source, and that they were created *Mod Tov*. There is embedded the glorious modern message that *every* person has built-in fundamental human rights (hence, also responsibilities).

Then, Will, many Christian thinkers, theologians, and activists looked to the example of Rabbi Yeshua spending his adult life teaching, healing the sick, and "hanging out with" outcasts: The poor, lepers, despised, women, children—those not considered by society and its leaders as being

Mod Tov. Will, those Christians took their inspiration from that Jewish Rabbi Yeshua and launched a multiple-pronged movement in many cultures and languages, in general, called "Liberation Theology." These Christian followers of Rabbi Yeshua did not spend their energy creating an abstract philosophy. No, they provided a rationale and inspiration that followed Rabbi Yeshua in actions that aimed at changing, not just individuals, but whole structures of society: One that would treat everyone as *Mod Tov.*

5. MALKUT SHOMAIM – THE "RULE OF HEAVEN"

Will, that Jewish rabbi was a pretty amazing guy! He put together and launched, not so much a theory, but an *action* plan that was at the same time deep, profoundly thought-through, as well as tested and worked-out in action. When you re-read the Gospels—which focus mainly on Rabbi *Yeshua*, not on *Christ* (that's St. Paul's special focus), on his teaching and his actions, that is, his putting his teaching into everyday *action*—you will notice a key term that he very frequently used: The *Reign of God.* You doubtless are asking yourself, "What in the world does that mean, especially in today's world?" Well, it again goes back to that pair of terms that describe both *everything* in the world as "good" (*Tov*), and all humans, as "very good" (*Mod Tov*).

Actually, Will, in the Hebrew language that Yeshua spoke, the term used was the "Rule of *Heaven*," *Malkut Shomaim*. Hmm, what do you think, Will? Do you agree that that's a little closer to our twenty-first century kind of language? Today we sometimes speak of "the heavens," meaning the cosmos, the universe (shades of our recent discovery of the Big Bang!). I think it suggests that there is a Heavenly order to the universe, cosmos, and that is what we humans should follow.

You know, Will, it's like the basic rules of ethics, which, as we saw in an earlier letter, if too many people in a community don't follow them, that society will destroy itself. For example, if everybody thought that it was OK to kill anybody they didn't like for one reason or another, pretty soon everybody would be dead except the "strongest" man, who would also eventually die. Then, what happens next, Will? Poof! That society is *Gone*!

Obviously, only those societies exist today which basically followed fundamental "do and don't" rules, like "Don't kill innocent persons"—the rest killed themselves off! Well, Will, you ask then: what was meant by Rabbi Yeshua's "*Rule* of Heaven," *Malkut Shomaim?*

6. MALKUT SHOMAIM – A FEMALE GOD?

Will, before I talk about how Yeshua understood this key term for him, *Malkut Shomaim*, because I know that you are something of a history buff, let me describe in passing a very interesting short video clip that I stumbled across on YouTube. It is about the very ancient use of the title *Malkut Shomaim* as it appeared in the fifth-century BCE Jewish colony in northern Egypt, Elephantine, and at the same time in Judea.

The interesting link is:

https://youtu.be/48TeNWCfHuA

Malkut Shomaim in Elephantine Judaism (a fortress state in northern Egypt settled by Jews) and in Judea of fifth-century BCE referred to a Jewish female God! Hence, at that time and place it meant not the "*Rule* of Heaven," but the "*Queen* of Heaven," later Christianized *Regina Coeli* in Latin, which you may well have sung in church!

Now Will, calm down! Yes, a lot of Jews in those ancient days did worship a female God! Just go get your Bible and turn to Jeremiah 44:15-19, where you see that the prophet roundly condemned those Jews who adored the female *Malkut Shomaim.* But the women stoutly stood their ground, saying to the Prophet that when they worshipped the *Queen of Heaven*, everything was just wonderful, thank you very much!

Of course, Will, things did not continue to go so well for them, and eventually Judaism fell into one political or military disaster after another. So, after the Jews were dragged into exile in Babylon in the fifth-century BCE, 70 years later they were allowed to return to Judea and put together the *Torah*, the Pentateuch, that is, the first five books of the Bible. And Will, from that time onward the whole Jewish population was committed to true monotheism. And so, also from then on

A Female God?

Malkut Shomaim was understood as the *Rule of Heaven*.

So now Will, let me go back to the question you put to me: "What was meant by Rabbi Yeshua's *Rule* of Heaven, *Malkut Shomaim*"?

Responding to that question somewhat completely would take a whole book or more. You will remember, Will, that we already touched on it in a way in our earlier letters. However, since we started today talking specifically about Yeshua being a Jew (and a rabbi to boot!), I pointed out that throughout his teaching we find him constantly coming back to this very Jewish idea and term of the "Rule of Heaven," *Malkut Shomaim.*

7. A TRANSFORMED PERSON AND SOCIETY

It was apparently a much-discussed issue in Yeshua's time for he is recorded having said about the *Malkut Shomaim*: "Some say 'it is here, some say that it is there!'" But no, Yeshua said that the "Rule of Heaven" is "*entos hymon.*" That's the original Greek of the Gospel. The second term, *hymon*, means "you." What is really interesting, Will, is that the term, *entos*, means *both* "within" *and* "among." In other words, Rabbi Yeshua was teaching that the "Rule of Heaven" is both *within* you and *among* you. You can see, Will, that Yeshua was making the dual point that you 1) needed to make the "Heavenly Rule" absolutely real *within* you. However, you could not follow the "Rule of Heaven" *only* individually, *entos*, "*within*" yourself, but it also needed to be 2) *entos*, "*among*," communally, yourselves!

So, you see, Will, Yeshua was pushing two very Jewish things: 1) Making human persons better one by one, *and* 2) working at changing the societal culture—increasingly fostering structures of society that will foster the "Rule of Heaven" so that *individual* persons will be taught and encouraged by the *community* to live within the *Malkut Shomaim*!

Think, Will, the first prayer that a Christian is taught is the so-called Lord's Prayer. It starts out: "Our Father who art in heaven (*Shomaim*), thy Kingdom (Rule, *Malkut*) come, thy will be done on Earth...." Of course, Will, the "Lord," after whom this quintessential Jewish prayer is named is none other than The Jew Rabbi Yeshua!

8. FOR GREEKS, THE BIG QUESTION WAS, WHAT TO THINK? FOR JEWS: WHAT TO DO?

Will, that emphasis by Rabbi Yeshua (I hope that by now you are beginning to *feel* comfortable with the fact that Yeshua was not a Christian but was a Jew!) leads us to notice that he was very, very different from the great Greek philosophers with whom we in the West are so familiar, like Socrates, Plato, and Aristotle. For them—and the Greek culture in general—the *big* question was: What should I *think*? One of the first things the Christians (by that time they were by far mostly Greek speakers/ thinkers) did when they gained freedom in the Roman Empire was to create, at the first Ecumenical (Universal) Council at Nicaea in 325 CE, a very detailed *Credo* (Latin, "I believe.") That is, Will, they hammered out what Christians should *think*.

Further, Will, let me ask you another question. I'm sure you know the answer:

what were the four faculties of the great medieval Christian universities founded upon in the High Middle Ages—like at Paris, Oxford, Cambridge, Bologna, and one of my Alma Mater's, Tubingen? The answer, of course, is Philosophy, Theology, Law, and Medicine. Notice, the first three were all about how we humans should *think*! And, if you didn't think the right way, you could be burned at the stake!

Will, let's have a little test: What is the Jewish *Credo*? I know that you know from visiting a number of synagogue services with Jewish friends. Before I remind you of the answer--we already spoke of it above--let me also recall that for centuries, traditional Jews have out a sense of respect avoided speaking out loud the *personal* name of God—*Yahweh* (which means: *I will be who I will be*)—but substitute for it the Hebrew word *Adonai*, Lord.

The answer, Will, as you've often heard recited, is *Shema Yisrael Adonai Eloheinu Adonai Echad!* "Remember O Israel, the Lord [*Yahweh*] our God, the Lord [*Yahweh*] is one." That's it! That's all you have to believe philosophically. However, there are hundreds of rules of *action* that you have to *do*. So, for the Greeks, the *big* (not the only) question was: "What must I *think*? But for the Jews, the *big* (not the only) question was: What must *I do*?

Will, I know that you have read at least part of the Gospels and have heard chunks of them read at the Christian services where you sang in your fantastic choirs. Think of what you know of the Gospels—not the letters of St. Paul and other parts of the New Testament. What are they about? The answer, of course, is that the four Gospels are all focused on Yeshua and his *teaching* and *actions*, helping....who? We saw, Will, that it was the marginalized; the outcasts of society. And what did he do with them? As seen above, we noted that he cured the sick, fed the hungry, and most of all, taught them that they were personally worthwhile (*Mod Tov*) and that they, whatever their place in life and society, should attempt to live the *Malkut Shomaim*, the "Rule of Heaven."

9. YESHUA'S TEACHING OF THE GOAL— MALKUT SHOMAIM

Will, every semester I teach a class on world religions. When I get to Christianity, I, of course, start with its founder, Rabbi Yeshua (I have to work a bit to get them used to making the connection between the terms Jesus and Yeshua!). I ask them, or at least the Christians in the class, "What did Yeshua say was the key to the reward for a good life?" They then usually come up with answers like, "Believe in Jesus as your Savior," "Avoid mortal sins," "Go to church on Sundays," etc., etc. Then I ask them, "Where is it recorded that Yeshua connected one or another of those things with, as he put it sometimes: Receive the reward, enter into heaven?" Of course, he didn't. Yeshua, as a *Mod Tov* Jew, said what, Will? Definitely "Not those who *say* 'Lord, Lord,' but those who *do* the will of my Father will enter into the reward that he has been prepared for you." And what is the "Will of my Father"? I quote

Yeshua directly: "Feed the hungry, give drink to the thirsty, clothe the naked, visit the sick, visit those in prison...."

Again, Will, it is very clear that Rabbi Yeshua was not a Greek, a Roman, a Persian, but an essential *Jew*, focusing not on what to believe or *think*, but on what to *do*, as the *big* question! Will, Yeshua, as a *Mod Tov* Jew, made it clear that "Not those who *say*, 'Lord, Lord,' but who *do* the will of my Father will live in the *Malkut Shomaim*!"

Again, Will, remember, one should not assume that Yeshua was saying, "Hang in there, things may be miserable for you now, but after you die, it will be just wonderful!" As we saw, he said that the *Malkut Shomaim* is "not *here* or *there*" (this life or afterlife), but is *entos hymon*, both within and among you—and you can make it starting *now* and *continuing*....

10. THE PICTURE LANGUAGE JEWS—AND RABBI YESHUA—USED: FATALLY MISUNDERSTOOD!

Will, you have read hundreds, and by now, probably thousands of books of all kinds, from serious ones to fantasy novels. Hence, by now you automatically recognize when some writing is to be taken at face value and others in some kind of expanded, transformed sense. Some writing is meant as factual, and some as metaphorical, or symbolic. Well, Will, I want to suggest that not everybody all the time recognized that difference that you do. Further, I want to point out that two thousand years ago when Yeshua lived, the vast majority of Jews could not read. Hence, if you wanted to influence them, you did not sit down and write books or newspaper articles (there were none then!). No, Will, you had to go out and tell stories that would capture the attention of the masses of unlettered persons (the Gospels tell of when Rabbi Yeshua taught crowds of several thousands!). The way I like to describe that way of speaking is to say that it tends to use *Picture Language*.

Will, that is precisely the sort of language Yeshua, as a good rabbi, used with the crowds of people who went to hear him teach. This was totally different from the way famous Greek philosophers spoke with their followers. They wrote many books (as far as we know, Rabbi Yeshua wrote zero!). They did not teach large crowds in great open spaces like Yeshua; rather, for example, the famous philosopher Plato created his *Akademia*; his equally famous student Aristotle was the head of the *Lykeion*. Both were places of scholarly thinking, writing, teaching of small groups of intellectuals—and whose names, *Academy* and *Lyceum*, we still use for institutions of higher learning.

Dear Will, as you know from your own reading, these and other Greek institutions were places of careful scientific and abstract philosophic thought—the very opposite of the way most of the Bible, as well as Jewish thought and writing in general, was carried out. For example, what do you suppose the Jew John the Baptist, a cousin of Yeshua, meant when, as recorded in the Fourth Gospel, one day he was talking with two of his disciples (i.e., students) and saw Yeshua walking by and said to them: "Look, the lamb of God." Do you suppose he meant that Yeshua was a white wooly four-legged animal? Of course not. You would say, the "lamb of God" must have had symbolic meaning to them—which the disciples understood, for they then immediately went and followed Rabbi Yeshua.

Or again, Will, what do you suppose Yeshua meant when he said to a group of Jews: "If your eye leads you astray, poke it out!"? Do you think that he meant that if any of his followers looked at something they shouldn't, they should actually poke their eye out!? Well, if so, there would be a lot more Christians with eyepatches in the world! Of course, he meant the poking metaphorically. Yeshua, like a good Jew, was speaking the way he knew the Jewish crowds were thinking—in *Picture Language*!

Will, you are probably thinking about now, "OK, Yeshua, and Jews in general, spoke in *Picture Language*—so?" The answer to "So?" is at first the obvious answer: If we want to understand what Rabbi Yeshua (and the Jewish Bible) meant in his teachings, we need to recognize that his teaching is couched in that kind of *Picture Language*, and not in either the concrete or abstract language the Greeks tended to use with such great depth.

Now, Will, I can hear you saying to yourself: Got it! Well, an awful lot of people—I really mean mainly Christians—didn't, and still don't, get it! For example, in one of the Gospels, it is recorded that some listener was really so impressed by Yeshua's teaching and actions that he said to him, "You are the son of God!" Wow! That sounds like this Jew meant that Yeshua was really a son of God— like a Greek would think that Apollo was "really" (or, to use a Greek-rooted technical term, ontologically) a son of the god Zeus. But, Will, we need to ask, is that what a Jew would mean by saying that "Yeshua was a son of God"? Not at all! When we read the Bible and other Jewish writings of the time, we find that to be a "son of God" meant that you are doing what God wants you to do—or, as was said in old-fashioned English, "you are a *godly* person."

This reading of Jewish *Picture Language* or *Ontological Language* as if it were *real,* is to badly *mis*read it—Yeshua did not go around saying "baaaa!" He did not mean to say what a Greek would *mis*understand--that he was a god like Apollo. Will, I can "hear" you going very silent, thinking about what a huge difference this makes in how to understand the Bible and all the teaching of Yeshua in a correct—Jewish!—way, if we want to "get it," and not to "get it wrong!"

11. SUMMARY

So, Will, we have really covered a lot of ground in this letter, which started with the question: What difference does it make that Yeshua was a rabbi? I pointed out that there were fundamental reasons why practically *everybody* should pay attention to the fact that Yeshua was a Jew. Then, Will, we saw that in the time of Yeshua the Jewish message of *one* God, *Echad*, who created everything, including *all* humans provided a basis for the development of the idea of *human rights* for all! In addition to the key term *Echad*, we looked at the important story at the very beginning of the Bible and saw that it said that everything that exists was created by God as "good," *Tov*, and that humans are "*very* good," *Mod Tov*. This provided another breakthrough notion eventually leading to the claim that *all* reality is *good*, and that all humans are not only good, *Tov*, but even very good, *Mod Tov*!

Summary

Then, Will, we began to focus on Rabbi Yeshua and saw that, because he took extremely seriously the Jewish notion that *all* humans are *Mod Tov*, he spent much of his teaching life hanging out with the outcasts of society precisely because he saw them as *Mod Tov*! Then, Will, we focused on another key term and insight of Yeshua, the "Rule of Heaven," *Malkut Shomaim*. We saw that it was no longer thought of as the *Queen of Heaven* (or, did it still secretly retain something of that feminine quality?), nor as some after-death heaven, but that it started here and now, and was both *in* you, and *among* you—*entos hymon*. This dual understanding of the *Rule of Heaven* taught that each person is *Mod Tov*, *very good*, and should be treated as such, both individually and through transformed societal structures which treated everyone as *Mod Tov*.

Related to that, Will, is the fact that for the Greeks the *big* question is "What must I *think?*" whereas the *big* question for Jews is "What must I *do?*" The answer for Jews was to follow the "Rule of Heaven," *Malkut Shomaim*. How? Each person followed this both *within* her/himself and *among*, societal structures, each other, thereby transforming each person and society as a whole.

Last, but by no means least, Will, we briefly investigated the critical issue of language. We saw that the Jewish language was fundamentally *Picture Language*, and was very different from the Greek language which tended to be abstract. This significant difference in the use of language, and how to properly to understand it, has frequently led to a *mis*understanding of what the Bible, and Rabbi Yeshua, taught and embodied.

So yes, Will, the fact that Jesus was a Jew, was Rabbi Yeshua, makes a hell—whoops, I mean, (Rule of) *Heaven* of a lot of difference!

Dein, Opa

www.ingramcontent.com/pod-product-compliance
Lightning Source LLC
Chambersburg PA
CBHW070049040426
42331CB00034B/2957